Everything
You Need
To Know

When a Brother or Sister Is Autistic

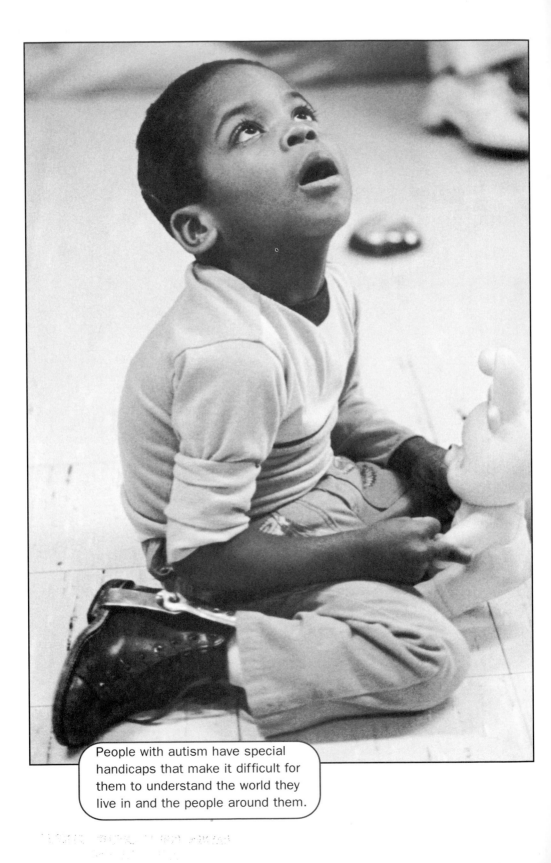

People with autism have special handicaps that make it difficult for them to understand the world they live in and the people around them.

Everything
You Need
To Know

When a
Brother or
Sister Is
Autistic

Marsha Sarah Rosenberg

THE ROSEN PUBLISHING GROUP, INC.
NEW YORK

Published in 2000 by The Rosen Publishing Group, Inc.
29 East 21st Street, New York, NY 10010

First Edition

Library of Congress Cataloging-in-Publication Data

Rosenberg, Marsha Sarah.
    Everything you need to know when a brother or sister is autistic /
Marsha Sarah Rosenberg.
        p.   cm. — (The need to know library)
    Includes bibliographical references and index.
    Summary: Discusses what autism is, how it is diagnosed and treated,
    and ways that siblings of people with autism can find support.
    ISBN 0-8239-3123-4
    1. Autism—Patients—Family relationships Juvenile literature.
  2. Autistic children—Family relationships Juvenile literature.
  3. Autism in children Juvenile literature.   [1. Autism.
  2. Mentally handicapped.] I. Title. II. Series.
  RJ506.A9R665 1999
  618.92'8982—dc21   99-26679
                                                 CIP

Manufactured in the United States of America

Contents

Introduction

Jacob was ten years old when his brother Noel was born. He thought that it would be great having a little brother around. Jacob hoped to teach Noel how to play baseball, build a snowman, and ride a bike someday. Little did he know that Noel would not grow up like other boys. Jacob might never have the opportunity to teach him all the things he had hoped. Some days Jacob feels that Noel doesn't even realize that he has an older brother.

Noel is five years old now and has never spoken a word. When Jacob tries to talk to him, it's almost as if Noel doesn't hear him or is ignoring him. Noel doesn't like to be held or cuddled and pulls away if anyone, including his parents, touches him even slightly. He has never made a *single friend in the neighborhood and likes it best when he is just left alone.*

For a few hours each day, Noel sits on the living room floor and rocks back and forth, staring into space as if he's daydreaming. Jacob bought Noel a train set for his last birthday, and Noel loves watching it go around and around the track. Sometimes he watches the train for hours without moving a muscle.

Noel likes his life to run on a schedule. There is a specific time to eat, sleep, and play. If he has to eat a little bit earlier or later than usual on a particular day, he gets very upset and throws a tantrum, making screaming and growling noises and sometimes even biting himself or banging his head against the wall. Noel never cries after hurting himself. Pain does not exist for him.

Often when the family goes on an outing, people who don't know Noel remark that he is behaving rudely or is strange. Jacob feels embarrassed by the way Noel acts and is sometimes too ashamed to have friends over to his house. Jacob knows, though, that his brother doesn't do the things he does on purpose. Jacob understands that Noel is autistic.

People with autism have special handicaps that make it difficult for them to understand the world they

Autism affects every aspect of a person's life and also affects the lives of the autistic person's family members.

live in and the people around them. Autism affects every aspect of a person's life and also places extreme demands on family members.

This book will tell you more about autism and the unusual world in which those with this disability live. It will also help you to better understand and cope with a brother or sister who is autistic.

Chapter One

What Is Autism?

Autism is a complicated and severe disability that usually appears during the first three years of life. It occurs in about fifteen of every 10,000 births and is four times more common in boys than in girls. Some people with autism are born with it, whereas others can develop normally until the age of two or three before symptoms appear. Autism can be found throughout the world in families of all racial, ethnic, social, and economic backgrounds.

Autism was first identified in 1943 by Dr. Leo Kanner, a child psychologist. He found that autism was the result of a neurological disorder that affects how the brain works, especially in the areas of social interaction and communication skills. In other words, Dr. Kanner found that autism affects the way in which a person relates to the world and the people in it. In

Autism is the third most common developmental disability in the United States.

Greek, the word "autism" literally means "selfism." This word is a good description of how people with the disability seem to live in a world of their own.

Over half a million people in the United States today have some form of autism, making it the third most common developmental disability. Autistic people look like anyone else without the disability, and that often makes it harder to promote awareness and understanding of the condition.

As Noel's family has learned, because autistic children look "normal," observers frequently assume that the children are just being naughty when they display unusual behaviors. Some people even blame the parents for not being able to control the child. This kind of reaction makes family members feel hurt and frustrated. That's one important reason to learn more about autism.

What Are the Characteristics of Autism?

Children with autism often appear to develop relatively normally, both physically and mentally, until they are between the ages of twenty-four and thirty months. At that time, parents may begin to notice delays in their child's language skills, play habits, or ability to interact with other people. Some autistic children do not speak at all; others make sounds or even say words. Most autistic children prefer to play alone, so many of them do not make friends.

An autistic child will almost never look for someone to be with or talk to. He or she will pay no attention to what other people are doing or feeling. Many autistic children repeat certain movements, such as rotating an object, flapping their arms, or biting their hands. Sometimes an autistic child will have an outburst of laughter or crying for no apparent reason.

The next two chapters discuss the characteristics and symptoms of autism as well as how this developmental disability can be diagnosed and treated.

Theory of Mind

Theory of mind is a relatively new idea in the study of autism. It says that many autistic people do not under-

Most autistic children prefer to play alone, so many of them do not make friends.

stand that other people have their own plans, thoughts, and points of view. It also says that autistic people may have trouble understanding the beliefs, attitudes, and emotions of other people.

If an autistic person does not understand that people all think differently, he or she will have a problem trying to speak to or make friends with other people. Autistic people don't understand what they are supposed to say or when they should say it. To them, being social is nothing but a huge and confusing mess.

What Causes Autism?

The causes of autism are still unknown, but much of the research being done today tells us that there may be multiple causes. It may be that the brain has abnormalities and doesn't function as it should or that there are imbalances in the central nervous system that cause the body to react in an unusual manner. Another theory is that there is a gene for autism that can be inherited, or passed down from one generation to the next in a family. Read on to find out more about these theories and about the research that is currently under way. A better understanding of the causes of autism is crucial, as it may lead to the development of possible cures for the disorder.

Chapter Two

Triad of Impairments

Triad of Impairments

People with autism are not usually physically handicapped; they do not need wheelchairs or canes, and they look just like anybody else. Rather, their major disabilities are mental. Certain characteristics are shared by all people with autism: They all have impairments related to communication skills, social interaction abilities, and imagination. This is referred to as the triad of impairments.

Communication Disorder

Communication disorder affects an autistic person's ability to interpret and use words, gestures, and facial expressions. Language skills develop slowly or, as in Noel's case, not at all. Those who are able to use language—about 50 percent—may use unusual words or phrases and may speak in a formal or flat voice. They may also repeat words, phrases, or sentences over and over again.

Most autistic people do not understand what other people are saying and cannot comprehend why people talk to one another. These problems make it extremely difficult for people with autism to communicate with others and to understand the outside world.

Problems with Social Interaction

One of the most typical symptoms of autism is a dysfunction (problem in functioning) in social behavior. Some autistic people avoid all forms of social interaction, choosing not to have any contact with other people. They may even throw a tantrum or run away if someone tries to talk to them.

This is not because people with autism don't like others or are fearful of them; rather, it is usually because they are hypersensitive to sensory stimuli. This means that these autistic individuals are very strongly affected by sights, sounds, smells, and touch (physical contact) in the outside world. A particular person's voice that sounds normal to most people may hurt the ears of someone with autism; a faint scent of perfume may be too strong for an autistic person to smell without feeling uncomfortable. This is probably the reason that Noel dislikes being held or cuddled.

Other autistic individuals are socially indifferent.

This means that they don't seem to mind being with people, but they don't mind being by themselves, either. Higher-functioning autistics often try very hard to make friends but have a difficult time keeping them. This is generally because they are unable to learn social skills.

Because autistic individuals can't understand that other people have their own thoughts, plans, and points of view, their conversations usually revolve around themselves. This can make people with autism seem self-centered, further adding to their difficulties in making friends.

Limited Imagination

Autistic children have problems developing play skills because they often have a limited range of imagination. They do not understand how to pretend and will have a hard time trying to play games with children their own age. This creates still more difficulty for them in relating to other people and forming friendships.

Other Typical Behaviors

In addition to the triad of impairments, other behaviors common in people with autism include stereotypy, hypersensitivity to the environment, and tunnel vision.

Stereotypy

Stereotypy, also known as self-stimulatory behavior or stimming, refers to repetitive movements of the body or of objects. It is typical of many develop-

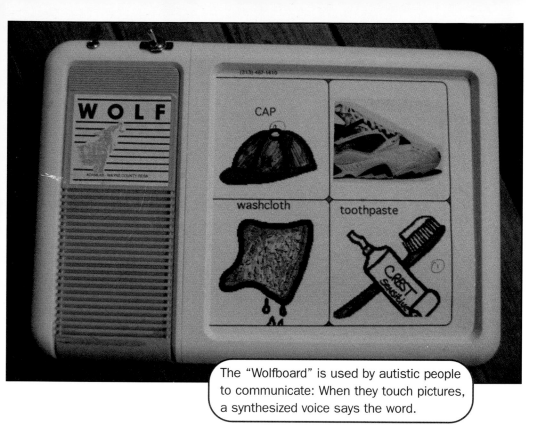

The "Wolfboard" is used by autistic people to communicate: When they touch pictures, a synthesized voice says the word.

mental disabilities but is most common in autism. Stereotypic behaviors include staring at lights, flapping the hands, snapping the fingers, rubbing or scratching the skin, rocking back and forth or from side to side, licking objects, biting the arms, and sniffing people. Researchers are still uncertain of the purpose of these behaviors. Some think that such actions may bring the autistic person some form of pleasure; others believe that the behaviors may help autistic individuals to block out everything going on around them.

Someone with autism might also display repetitive behavior by strictly following the same routine every day. This person's days may be scheduled in a highly specific order: eating, dressing, sleeping, and doing other activities at exactly the same time and in exactly the same way every day. Sometimes if outside forces prevent the autistic person from following a particular routine, he or she may become very distressed, throwing a tantrum or stimming to show frustration and unhappiness.

Associated Problems

People diagnosed with autism may have problems with sleeping, eating, and using the toilet. They are often more likely to develop allergies and food sensitivities than the average person because of their impaired immune systems. Other characteristic behaviors include laughing, crying, or giggling at inappropriate times. Many people with autism seem to be unaware of pain, heat, or cold.

Autistic people may show aggressive or violent behavior, sometimes even injuring themselves. This is called self-injurious behavior; it refers to any behavior that causes someone to inflict (bring about) physical harm on him- or herself, such as bruises, scratches, and open wounds. Autistics may injure themselves as a result of head banging, hand biting, or excessive scratching or rubbing. Sometimes self-injurious behavior occurs because of pain or frustration. Other times it may occur because it brings the person some kind of inner pleasure.

If outside forces prevent an autistic person from following a particular routine, he or she may become very distressed.

As mentioned earlier in this chapter, some autistic children become afraid or confused or feel pain as a result of certain sounds that they hear or things that they see. This is called sensory oversensitivity, and it can vary in degree from slight to severe. If an autistic child puts his hands over his ears, it may mean that he is oversensitive to noise. If he flicks his fingers in front of his eyes, he is likely to have visual sensitivity problems. Autistic children with severe sensory over-sensitivities will often have tantrums or behave badly in supermarkets or shopping malls because of sensory overload. The huge variety of sounds and images taking place all around them is just too overwhelming to tolerate.

Because the environment as a whole may be too much for certain autistic children to endure, they may try to ignore or block out their surroundings by focusing on only one small part of the world, acting as if nothing else exists. This type of blocking-out behavior is known as tunnel vision. Parents often mistakenly think that their autistic child is deaf because when the child is in this mode of behavior, he or she shows no response to any type of loud noise; this can include the earsplitting sound of two pots being banged together behind the child's head.

There are great differences in behavior among people with autism. Some who are mildly affected may show only slight delays in learning to use language but may have greater difficulty with social interaction. Some autistics have average or even above average verbal and memory skills, but they may find it difficult to use their imagination while playing games with others.

People often assume that just because someone has autism, he or she does not laugh, smile, make eye contact, or show affection. This is not true. Like other people, autistics respond to their environment in both positive and negative ways. They can and do show a variety of emotions; in some cases, their autistic behaviors may change or even disappear over time.

Chapter Three

Diagnosis and Treatment of Autism

There are no blood tests, X rays, or any other type of medical examination that can show who has autism and who does not. Professionals who are familiar with the disorder diagnose autism by spending time with the child and watching how he or she communicates, responds to others, and reacts to the environment. The earlier the diagnosis is made, the more likely it is that the autistic child will benefit from treatment.

How Is Autism Diagnosed?

It is best that autism be diagnosed by a team of professionals, usually consisting of a psychologist, a child psychiatrist, a speech therapist, and a social worker. These team members base their findings on observations of the child's behavior. They consult with parents and ask

There is no "typical" person with autism, and there are differences in the behavior of each autistic child.

about the child's early developmental history to find out if he or she has any delayed or unusual language patterns, problems with social interaction, stimming behaviors, or sensory oversensitivity. It is important for this team to distinguish autism from other conditions, since autism can easily be mistaken for mental retardation, a behavior disorder, or hearing problems.

There is no "typical" person with autism, and there are differences in the behavior of each autistic child. Therefore, it is very important that professionals form a proper diagnosis so that appropriate programs and treatments can begin as soon as possible. Early intervention will help the autistic child to reach his or her maximum potential in life.

Is There a Cure for Autism?

Autism, like most developmental disabilities, has no cure. To cure someone with autism would mean to restore his or her brain to perfect health and to make that person's internal world function normally. From what is now understood about the complexity of brain disorders, a cure seems unrealistic. However, doctors and scientists are always finding better ways to understand autism and to help people cope with and treat the symptoms of the disability.

With appropriate intervention, many of the typical behaviors of autism can be changed to more positive and healthy behaviors—even to the point that some children or adults may no longer show any visible signs of the disorder. The majority of autistics, however, continue to have symptoms of the disability throughout their lives.

How Can People with Autism Be Helped?

Although there is no known cure for autism, it is a treatable disability. Research continues into both causes and treatments of this disorder. Studies have shown that people with autism can improve remarkably with proper instruction. They can eventually become more responsive to others as they learn to understand the world around them. The following are

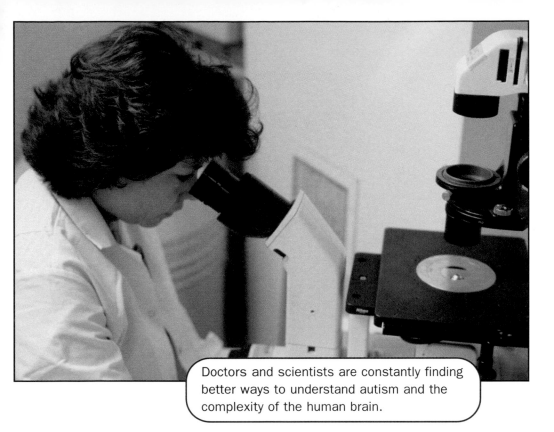

Doctors and scientists are constantly finding better ways to understand autism and the complexity of the human brain.

some effective approaches and treatments for people diagnosed with autism.

Behavior Modification

This technique can be used by parents, teachers, and therapists. It aims to change abnormal behavior by relaxing the autistic individual's fears and anxieties about outside sensory stimuli. This is achieved using positive reinforcement.

For example, if an autistic child is expected to say a specific word or behave in a certain way, a reward such as a piece of cereal or fruit is given to the child each time he or she says the word or performs the behavior. In this way, the child is rewarded for performing properly, mak-

Studies have shown that people with autism can improve remarkably with proper instruction.

ing it much more likely that this child will continue to do and learn the behaviors that are expected of him or her.

Speech Therapy

Through this process, a speech or language therapist (someone who specializes in treating speech and language difficulties) helps an autistic person to develop his or her communication skills. The therapist aids in expanding the person's vocabulary and teaches him or her how to follow directions.

The speech therapist also shows the autistic person the proper uses of different words. Sometimes this type of therapy is done in groups that bring together many people with communication or language disabilities.

This helps the autistic person improve his or her ability to interact with others.

Sensory Integration

Our senses allow us to experience, interpret, and respond to different things in our environment. Someone with autism may be over- or underresponsive to certain sensory stimuli and may react to certain sights, sounds, smells, or touches with frustration, aggression, or withdrawal. An occupational therapist or physical therapist can treat symptoms such as these with a process called sensory integration.

Through this process, the therapist exposes the autistic individual to gradually increasing amounts of sensory stimuli, thus helping the patient to organize the use of his or her senses. For instance, an autistic child who cannot tolerate light may start off therapy in a setting with very dim lighting. With each passing session, the brightness of the light will continue to increase so that the autistic person can slowly become used to higher and higher intensities of light.

Music Therapy

Music is an effective treatment for some of the behavior problems associated with autism because it is a non-threatening and largely nonverbal form of communication. A music therapist or teacher may use songs with simple words or repetitive phrases to assist an autistic person in developing language and social interaction skills. Everyone responds positively to at least some kind of music, and some autistic children who do not speak at all nevertheless love to sing. In fact, autistic children often show unusual sensitivities to music, and some have been noted to play instruments with exceptional talent.

Social Stories

A technique created by Carol Gray, social stories present appropriate social behaviors in the form of a story. Since social interaction may not come naturally to the autistic person, stories like these provide answers to the who, what, when, where, and why of social situations. This helps the autistic person understand how to interact with others in the real world.

Medications

Several medications can be given to autistic people that have an obvious and dramatic effect on behavior. Melatonin, a natural sleeping aid, has proved to be remarkably effective for restless autistic children who have a hard time getting to sleep. Vitamin B_6 and magnesium treatment has also shown a wide range of benefits when given to autistic children: Their eye contact improves, they exhibit less stimming behaviors, they throw fewer tantrums, and they show more interest in the world around them.

The hormone secretin is a relatively new treatment for the symptoms of autism. It appears to cause dramatic improvements in speech and language. Naltrexone is another drug used in the treatment of autism; its positive effects include increased socialization, reduction of self-injurious behaviors, and increased general happiness.

People with autism have very sensitive nervous systems and may require much lower doses of medications than people with normal nervous systems. Medications designed to treat the symptoms of autism should be prescribed by a doctor and given carefully to avoid harmful side effects.

Dietary Intervention

There is growing evidence that many people with autism are sensitive to certain foods such as grains and dairy products. This type of food allergy can cause or worsen headaches, stomachaches, bed wetting, stuttering, excessive whining and crying, sleeplessness, aggression, fatigue (extreme tiredness), depression, and other related problems. The best way to stop a reaction to a particular food substance is to remove that food from the person's diet.

Physical Exercise

One of the most neglected yet effective treatments for autistic individuals is exercise. Studies have shown that vigorous or strenuous exercise is often associated with decreases in stimming behaviors, aggression, self-injurious behaviors, and destructiveness. Since physical exercise is inexpensive, safe, and healthy, it makes sense to try an exercise program to reduce behavior problems before using more potent treatments such as drugs.

A Balanced Approach

These are only a few of the effective approaches and treatments for people diagnosed with autism. A well-designed intervention approach for the treatment of this disability should include some level of each therapy mentioned previously.

In addition, a good program will provide training and support not only for the autistic individual but for caregivers as well. Services such as pre-school programs, counseling, and training for family members can provide this type of support.

Students with autism should receive training in vocational and community living skills beginning at the earliest possible age. Learning to cross a street, make a simple purchase, or ask for assistance are very important skills that will help the autistic person to feel independent and will give him or her the opportunity for more personal choice and freedom in the community. The best way to help people with autism is to give them the time, patience, and understanding they need to make sense out of the confusing world they live in.

Chapter Four

The Spectrum Disorder

Autism is often referred to as the spectrum disorder; this name reflects the fact that the symptoms and characteristics of this disability come in a wide variety of combinations and range from mild to severe. Two children who are both diagnosed with autism can behave very differently from each other.

Professionals use a handbook called the *Diagnostic and Statistical Manual,* fourth edition (*DSM-IV*) to diagnose both autism and several autism-related disorders that include some but not all of the characteristics of autism. There are many more children with autistic-like disorders than with autism itself. Here is a short list of some of these disorders.

Asperger's Disorder

Individuals with this disorder usually speak very well and use proper grammar and vocabulary. Their voices tend to be flat and emotionless, however, and their conversations usually revolve around themselves. Many have above average IQs and are obsessed with topics such as music, history, and the weather. They show odd forms of stimming behavior, but their sensory problems are not as dramatic as those of people with other forms of autism.

Rett's Disorder

This disorder affects mostly females and involves autistic-like behaviors such as sleeping problems, hand flapping, and repetitive rocking of the body. Many people with this disorder are severely mentally retarded, have breathing difficulties, and experience seizures, or sudden attacks that cause the body to twist and jerk.

Landau-Kleffner Syndrome

People with this syndrome are commonly males who either gradually or suddenly lose their language abilities between the ages of three and seven. A typical autistic-like characteristic of this disorder is the failure to respond to sounds. In fact, many parents may at first suspect that their child has lost his or her hearing. Individuals with this disability do not seem to feel pain, can be aggressive, and need to follow a specific routine every day.

Angelman Syndrome

Individuals suffering from this disorder show many of the behaviors that are characteristic of autism, such as hand flapping, little or no speech, hyperactivity, and sleeping or eating problems. Some may bite or pull hair. In contrast to those with autism, people with this syndrome are often very sociable and affectionate and love to laugh.

Prader-Willi Syndrome

This disorder is characterized by an obsession with food, which causes many people with this syndrome to be overweight. Like autistics, individuals with Prader-Willi syndrome usually exhibit delayed language development, learning disabilities, sleep disturbances, skin picking, temper tantrums, and a high tolerance for pain.

The Autistic Savant

Autistic savants are individuals with autism who have extraordinary skills and talents. Before 1978, these individuals were labeled "idiot savants" because they were uneducated in many areas but savants, or geniuses, in others. Dr. Bernard Rimland introduced the term "autistic savant," which we use today.

There are many forms of savant abilities. The most common are mathematical calculations, artistic or musical abilities, and remarkable memory skills. For instance, you may ask an autistic person with calendar memory to tell you what day of the week March 28, 1969, fell on. Within seconds, he or she will come up with the correct answer.

Some are able to recall every fact about each of the United States presidents; others can multiply, divide, and find square roots of large numbers in their head in a matter of moments. Many performers with autism have a great memory for music. In some cases, a person can hear a piece of music only once and play it back in its entirety.

The movie *Rain Man* introduced autism and the autistic savant to millions of people. In the film, Raymond, played by Dustin Hoffman, shows his memory skills by rattling off ballplayer statistics, memorizing names and numbers in the telephone book, and counting cards in Las Vegas. As a result of this movie, some people believe that all autistic people have these abilities. In reality, only 10 percent of those diagnosed with autism are savants.

The movie *Rain Man* introduced autism and the autistic savant to millions of people.

Some autistic adults live and work independently in the community.

The Possibility of Seizures During Puberty

About one in four autistic individuals begins to experience seizures during puberty, the time when a child's body starts to mature. The reason for these seizures is not yet known. One possible cause is the vast hormonal changes that take place in the body during adolescence.

Sometimes these seizures are noticeable, but often they are small and not easily recognized. Most autistic individuals do not experience seizures during puberty. In fact, during this time they usually make great strides in improving their symptoms with proper treatment and guidance. It is important to be aware of the possibility of seizures, however, because if untreated, seizures can be dangerous to the body and brain.

Autistic Adults

Adults with autism live in a variety of settings, including group homes or apartments, structured residential facilities, or at home with family members. Some autistic adults live and work independently in the community, whereas others need the support of their families and trained professionals. Adults with autism can benefit from vocational training, in which they learn a specific job or skill. They can also benefit from social and recreational programs that teach them how to interact with others. Some adults with autism are currently working as successful artists, painters, farm workers, office workers, and computer operators.

Chapter Five

When Your Brother or Sister Is Autistic

There are over 5.8 million children in the United States with disabilities. Many of these children have brothers and sisters just like you. As the sibling of someone with a disability, you likely share many of the same concerns as a parent of a disabled child.

You have probably experienced many different feelings about your sibling's disability. The next few chapters discuss some of these feelings and what you should know if you have a brother or sister who is autistic. You will also read about how you can help your autistic sibling while helping yourself to better understand this disorder.

Being a Teenager with an Autistic Sibling

The teen years involve huge physical and emotional changes that can make even the most confident people wonder whether they will ever really fit in. Many teens are deeply insecure about their identity and try very hard to act or dress a certain way in order to be accepted. Having a sibling with a disability can bring additional difficulties to the challenge of fitting in.

As a teen with an autistic sibling, you probably have some conflicting feelings about your brother or sister. You may not be particularly proud of some of these emotions. These feelings are normal and happen even in sibling relationships that do not involve a disability. Arguments and fights between brothers and sisters are natural and occur in normal families everywhere. Actually, the presence of conflict is a healthy sign because it shows that you are treating your autistic sibling just as you would a brother or sister who did not have a disability.

Being an adolescent means that you are beginning to discover yourself as someone independent from your family. You want to form your own group of friends with whom you can share your thoughts and feelings. If you have a sibling who is autistic, it may be difficult to find friends who can share your unique experiences.

You may also be embarrassed to bring friends to your home for fear of what they might say or think when they find out that you have a disabled brother or sister. Or maybe you resent the amount of responsibility you have for your brother or sister that keeps you from doing all of the things you want to do.

Here are a few other feelings you may be experiencing if you have a brother or sister who is autistic:

Isolation

You may feel that you are not being given vital information about your sibling or that you are being left out of important decisions. You may also feel ignored by the professionals who are helping your sibling.

Guilt

You may believe that you somehow caused your sibling's disability, or you may feel guilty that your sibling is disabled, whereas you are perfectly healthy.

Resentment

You may become angry or frustrated when your sibling with special needs becomes the focus of your family's attention and is allowed to behave in ways that would normally be unacceptable.

Pressure

You may feel that you need to be an overachiever in school, sports activities, or in your behavior to make up for the abilities that your sibling lacks. You may also feel pressured to take care of your autistic brother or sister more than you would a normal sibling. Perhaps you fear that you will become your sibling's only caregiver when he or she gets older and that you will not be able to lead a life of your own.

You don't need to be an overachiever in school, sports activities, or in your behavior to make up for the abilities that your sibling lacks.

In addition to experiencing the feelings listed previously, you may feel helpless to improve your sibling's condition. You may feel irritable, have difficulty concentrating, feel frustrated, or have trouble eating or sleeping. These are all feelings that many brothers and sisters of autistic siblings share. It is important to know that you are not alone. It is also vital that you learn all you can about the disorder and what you can do to reduce some of your worries about being the brother or sister of a sibling diagnosed with autism.

What You Need to Know

It is necessary to understand that each autistic person is different and has his or her own variety of characteristics. It is also vital to know the truth about certain common myths (false beliefs) associated with autism.

- Autism is not a mental illness, although autism and mental retardation often appear together in individuals.

- Children with autism are not badly behaved kids who choose to act inappropriately.

- Autism is not caused by bad parenting.

- Autism is not contagious. You cannot develop symptoms of it just by hanging around autistic people.

What You Can Do to Help

We've all had especially good teachers who have helped us achieve success. It is entirely possible for you to become such a teacher for your autistic sibling. You can help your sibling learn about the world by teaching him or her good manners, how to share, and how to take turns. With patience and understanding of the different way in which autistic people think, you can help your brother or sister to discover his or her surroundings and make yourself a significant part of your sibling's learning experiences.

Many people with autism think visually. This means that they do not think in words, but rather in pictures. Knowing this, you can come up with special ways of teaching your sibling new ideas.

For instance, if you want to teach your autistic brother or sister words like "above" and "below," you might show him or her what these words "look" like. One way would be to hold a book over a table and repeat several times that the book is above the table. Then hold the book under the table, stating several times that the book is now below the table. Flashcards are another useful teaching tool because they help the learner to associate words with pictures.

If your autistic sibling is good at drawing or likes to type on the computer, you might want to encourage these abilities by spending time with your brother or

Because many people with autism think visually, you can make an effort to communicate with pictures rather than words.

sister as he or she participates in these activities. Doing this can help your sibling to develop new abilities, such as learning better language skills. If, like Noel, your autistic brother or sister likes trains, you can help him or her learn more about them by reading aloud a picture book on trains. You could even do math problems or teach new words using trains.

Some autistic people dislike certain sounds because they hurt their ears. The sound of a vacuum cleaner or chairs scraping across the floor can lead to a tantrum or aggressive behavior in some autistic individuals. The best thing to do is to keep this kind of painful noise away from your sibling as much as possible. Preventing your sibling from becoming overwhelmed by sensory stimuli will make life much easier for both of you.

Another way to improve communication with your sibling is to sing or speak in a low whisper to him or her when you have something to say. These are pleasant sounds that are not as frightening or painful to the autistic person's ear as regular speech.

These are just a few of the things you can do to help your autistic sibling become connected to the world. Remember to focus on the abilities, not the disabilities. Encourage your brother or sister to be the best he or she can be. Showing your sibling that he or she is loved, and being able to watch him or her learn new things, is not only a great experience for your sibling but a rewarding one for you, too.

Chapter Six

What About Me?

Opportunities for Personal Growth

As the sibling of an autistic person, you have many more opportunities for personal growth and character development than do many other people whose siblings do not have a disability. The following are some of these special opportunities.

Maturity

When a brother or sister is born with autism, the whole family often works together as a team to help the child develop and learn about the outside world. When this happens, you have the opportunity to begin acting at an adult level, using your reasoning and senses to become much more aware of the disability and about life itself. Because of the special experiences—both good and bad—that you will share with your sibling, your level of maturity will become greater than that of other people your age.

Social Competence

Social competence refers to your ability to get along with others in the world. Siblings of autistic individuals are often more willing to talk to people and strike up conversations. This is probably because the brother or sister of an autistic individual learns to ask questions and to seek knowledge from doctors and other professionals about his or her sibling's condition.

Insight

Being the brother or sister of an autistic person makes you better able to feel sympathy for the pain and suffering of others, as well as more appreciative of the fact that you are not disabled. Each day becomes more special than the one before, leaving you constantly amazed at the gifts of life.

Tolerance

Siblings of autistic individuals are often more accepting than their peers of many different types of people. This is usually because their experiences have made them appreciate the beauty of difference. Sometimes it is because they have seen others taunt and tease their

Being a sibling of an autistic individual may make you more willing to talk to people and strike up conversations.

sibling, making them understand how painful intolerance can be.

Pride

When an autistic brother or sister learns something new, you feel a sense of pleasure and satisfaction about his or her accomplishment. You feel proud of your role as a member of a family that helps to contribute to the mental, physical, and emotional growth of your sibling.

Loyalty

If you have a brother or sister who is autistic, you probably fight with him or her occasionally, just like normal siblings. However, you may also feel a very strong bond with that sibling as well as a sense of loy- alty and protection toward him or her. Because you know how difficult it is for your sibling to make sense of the world, you will most likely feel the need to defend him or her if someone teases or makes nega- tive remarks.

Advocacy

Advocacy, or speaking up for the rights and dignity of others, may come naturally to some people with autistic brothers or sisters. Others, however, may be uncomfort- able with it. Advocating requires being assertive and speaking openly about the special needs of a person. Parents are often role models for advocacy and teach their nonautistic children that it is okay to explain and express themselves, or even to be assertive when sup- porting their autistic brother or sister.

As an advocate, you can explain to someone who doesn't know much about autism that your sibling has a brain disorder that causes him or her to rock back and forth, not be able to speak, or dislike change in his or her daily routine. You can inform the person that it is all right to ask questions about the disorder and that there is nothing to fear.

Chapter Seven

Helping Yourself

Within a family, siblings will more than likely spend as much time as the mother or father with an autistic brother or sister. Sibling relationships are usually the longest lasting relationships in families, and those with an autistic brother or sister will face concerns about the disability for most of their lives. Many siblings of autistic individuals grow up without helpful support programs or good sources of information about the disability. These siblings can become frustrated and confused by a disorder they do not understand.

Educating Yourself

As the brother or sister of an autistic person, you will have a lifelong and ever changing need for information. You will need to know what the disability is and what to

As the brother or sister of an autistic person, you will have to educate yourself about autism.

expect. Parents, professionals, and specialized agencies should be able to provide you with much of the information you need. You and your parents must keep communication lines open and set aside time for each other. This will help the whole family to share their concerns about the disability and to be reassured that each member of the family is there for one another. This will also give you, as a sibling, the opportunity to express your positive and negative feelings about autism and help you to cope with stressful events involving your brother or sister.

Some professionals and care providers need to be reminded that there is more to a family than just the autistic child and his or her parents. They must get the message that you are an active member of your family and that you do not want to be excluded. It would benefit you to attend classes and visit clinics that can provide you with answers to your questions. By doing this, you can hear other opinions and perspectives on the disorder that will keep you well informed about the many aspects of autism.

Peer Support

Many parents of autistic children get support and helpful information from other parents who are in a similar situation. Unfortunately many siblings of autistic children "go it alone," without the benefit of knowing someone their age who can relate to what they are feeling and experiencing.

Parents of autistic children can get support and information from other parents who are in a similar situation

Brothers and sisters need to know that they are not alone in their concerns. Participation in a group for siblings of disabled brothers or sisters allows you to meet others who are in similar circumstances. Groups such as these can provide you with a chance to discuss feelings that are difficult to express to family members or even to admit to yourself.

Sibshops

Sibshops are best described as opportunities for brothers and sisters of autistic individuals to get peer support in a fun, recreational setting. Sometimes sibshops are more like events that celebrate the many contributions made by the brothers and sisters of those with special needs. Sibshop activities include fun and games that may relieve some of the stress that comes with having a disabled sibling.

Attending a sibshop can provide you with the opportunity to meet other people who have autistic siblings and can also give you the chance to discuss your feelings and concerns about your particular sibling. By sharing your thoughts and experiences with others in a relaxed environment, you can learn how to handle situations that many other siblings of autistic individuals deal with. You may make lasting friendships with people who, like you, understand the ups and downs of life. You may even begin to appreciate some of the positive aspects of having an autistic sibling that were discussed earlier.

The Children's Sibling Support Project maintains a database of over 200 sibshops and other sibling programs within the United States. You can contact this organization to find out if there is a program in your area. If there isn't one near you, it can assist you in starting one. For information on how to contact the Children's Sibling Support Project, check out the Where to Go for Help section at the back of this book.

Being the brother or sister of someone with autism can teach you how to love without expecting affection in return. It can also teach you that no one is perfect and that each of us has our own strengths and weaknesses. Most important, it can show you that human value is not measured by how smart or attractive you are. Being the brother or sister of an autistic person makes *you* pretty special too.

Glossary

autistic savant An autistic individual who has extraordinary talent that most normal people do not have.

central nervous system The part of the nervous system, consisting of the brain and spinal cord, that coordinates the activity of the entire nervous system.

child psychiatrist / psychologist A doctor who deals with mental disorders in children.

developmental disability A physical or mental handicap that prevents or slows normal development.

Diagnostic and Statistical Manual, fourth edition (DSM-IV) A handbook used by most professionals to diagnose mental disorders.

dysfunction A failure to function normally.

hypersensitive Being very easily affected by sensory stimuli in the surrounding environment.

impairment A problem or difficulty with something.

occupational therapist A person trained to help individuals recover from certain illnesses by having them participate in creative activities designed for this purpose.

physical therapist A person trained to treat disease, injury, deformity, or weakness with massage and exercise.

puberty The stage at which a child's body begins to mature.

reinforcement A type of reward for performing a desired behavior, increasing the probability that it will occur again in the future.

sensory oversensitivity (sensory overload) Fear, confusion, or pain that results from an overload of sensory stimuli.

sensory stimuli Seeing, hearing, smelling, and touching sensations received from the outside world.

social worker A person trained to help individuals with difficulties in various aspects of their lives, including health-related problems.

speech therapist A specialist who provides treatment to improve defects of speech.

Where to Go for Help

For further information or to learn more about the treatments, programs, and services available for autistic individuals and their families, contact the following groups:

In the United States

Autism Network International
P.O. Box 448
Syracuse, NY 13210-0448
Web site: http://www.students.uiuc.edu/~bordner/ani

Autism Research Institute
4182 Adams Avenue
San Diego, CA 92116
Web site: http://www.autism.com/ari/

Where to Go for Help

Autism Society of America
7910 Woodmont Avenue, Suite 300
Bethesda, MD 20814-3015
(800) 328-8476
Web site: http://www.autism-society.org/

CAN—The Cure Autism Now Foundation
5225 Wilshire Boulevard, Suite 226
Los Angeles, CA 90036
(323) 549-0500
e-mail: CAN@primenet.com

Center for the Study of Autism
P.O. Box 4538
Salem, OR 97302
Web site: http://www.autism.org

Federation for Children with Special Needs
1135 Tremont Street, Suite 420
Boston, MA 02120
(617) 236-7210
Web site: http://www.fcsn.org

The Children's Sibling Support Project
Children's Hospital and Medical Center
P.O. Box 5371, CL-09
Seattle, WA 98105
(206) 368-4911

Web site: http://www.chmc.org/sibsupp/

In Canada

Association for the Neurologically Disabled of Canada
Clinic locations in Toronto, Montreal, and Regina.
Call or e-mail for specific addresses.
(800) 561-1497
Web site: http://www.and.ca
E-mail: info@and.ca

Autism Society of Ontario
1 Greensboro Drive, Suite 306
Etobicoko, ON M9W 1C8
(418) 246-9592
Web site: http://www.autismsociety.on.ca

Autism Treatment Services of Canada
404 94th Avenue, SE
Calgary, AB T2J 0E8
(403) 253-6961
Web site: http://www.autism.ca

Web Sites

Autism: Family Village
http://www.familyvillage.misc.edu/lib_autm.htm

Autism Resources
http://www.autism-info.com/

For Further Reading

Gartenberg, Zachary. *Mori's Story: A Book About a Boy with Autism.* Minneapolis, MN: Lerner Publications, 1998.

Kaufman, Barry Neil. *A Miracle to Believe In.* New York: Fawcett Books, 1994.

Martin, Ann. *Kristy and the Secret of Susan.* Madison, WI: Demco Media, 1990.

Maurice, Catherine. *Let Me Hear Your Voice: A Family's Triumph over Autism.* New York: Fawcett Books, 1994.

O'Neill, Jasmine Lee. *Through the Eyes of Aliens: A Book About Autistic People.* Philadelphia, PA: Jessica Kingsley Publications, 1998.

Werlin, Nancy. *Are You Alone on Purpose?* Boston, MA: Houghton Mifflin Co., 1994.

A valuable and informative newsletter for children and adults with autism:

The Morning News
Carol Gray, Editor
Jenison Public School
2140 Bauer Road
Jenison, MI 49428

Index

Index

About the Author

Marsha S. Rosenberg is a freelance editor and writer living and working in New Jersey. This is her first book for young adults.

Photo Credits

Cover shot © Skjold. Pp. 2, 8, 10, 17, 19, 26, 36, 44 © Photo Researchers, Inc.; pp. 12, 23 © The Image Works; p. 25 by Seth Dinnerman; p. 35 © The Everett Collection, Inc.; pp. 41, 48 by Ira Fox; p. 51 by Brian Silak; p. 53 by Les Mills.